THINGS
WE
DO

THINGS
WE
DO

by
Sylvia Vardell & Janet Wong

So much to do!
Enjoy & be sure to
WAVE!
Janet Clare
Fagal

Pomelo
Books

100% of the profits from this book
will be donated
to the IBBY Children in Crisis Fund

IBBY CHILDREN IN CRISIS

The IBBY Children in Crisis Fund provides support for children whose lives have been disrupted through war, civil disorder, or natural disaster. The program gives immediate support and help – and also aims for long-term community impact, aligning with IBBY's goal of giving every child the right to become a reader.

ibby.org/awards-activities/activities/ibby-children-in-crisis-fund

usbby.org/donate.html

Pomelo Books
4580 Province Line Road
Princeton, NJ 08540
PomeloBooks.com
info@pomelobooks.com

Text/compilation copyright © 2021 by Pomelo Books. All rights reserved.
Individual poems copyright © 2021 by the individual poets. All rights reserved.
Photos sourced from Canva.com and iStockphoto.com.

Library of Congress Cataloging-in-Publication Data is available.

ISBN 978-1-937057-30-5

Please visit us:
PomeloBooks.com

POEMS BY

Beth Brody

Joseph Bruchac

Jen Bryant

Mary E. Cronin

Linda A. Dryfhout

Margarita Engle

Janet Clare Fagal

Marilyn Garcia

Nikki Grimes

Carol Labuzzetta

Marty Lapointe-Malchik

Grace Lin

Molly Lorenz

Jone Rush MacCulloch

Pat Mora

Linda Sue Park

Moe Phillips

Jack Prelutsky

Janice Scully

Linda Kulp Trout

Padma Venkatraman

Carole Boston Weatherford

Leslie Stall Widener

Janet Wong

Jane Yolen

Helen Kemp Zax

Janet Clare Fagal
P. 53
"W"

TABLE OF CONTENTS

ASK

by Janet Wong

When questions start bouncing
around in my head,
my hand shoots up in the air.
Who? What? When? Where?
Why did it happen? And *how?*

I **ask** my mouth to be quiet.
I **ask** my mind to calm down.
But my mouth and my mind
keep on wondering – and
they want some answers NOW!

BEND

by Beth Brody

I trust my body
To bend the way I need it to
To show I'm strong
To help me breathe
To open up my heart.

CLAP

by Joseph Bruchac

Clap, clap, clap your hands
Clap your hands together.

Clap, clap, clap your hands
In fair or stormy weather.

Clap, clap, clap your hands
Clap them when you're singing.

Clap, clap, clap your hands
When fun things are beginning.

Clap, clap, clap your hands
When the frogs are peeping.

Just don't clap your hands
When someone else is sleeping.

D

DANCE

by Nikki Grimes

Look! The sun rises
on the tips of her toes,
then leaps impossibly high.
She's a golden ballerina
with cloud friends
who pirouette across the sky.
"My turn!" I squeal
as I whirl, and twirl,
hands sweeping the air.
Reaching for happy
on days when I'm sad,
I dance without a care!

E

EAT

by Jack Prelutsky

I do not need my ears to EAT,
My elbows or my eyes.
If I should need my ankles,
It would come as a surprise.

I do not need my knees to EAT,
My shoulders or my toes.
But when I EAT, I need my mouth . . .
It's underneath my nose.

F

FLY

by Carole Boston Weatherford

I had a dream last night
that I was in free flight
above the tallest tower,
high on my own power.

I landed in my bed,
the thrill still in my head.

If only dreams were true,
I'd soar up in the blue.
I have no wings, but wish I might.
Until then, I'll **fly** my kite.

GROW

by Jane Yolen

Some kids grow *fast*
Some kids grow s l o w
Some kids just twist like a v ᵢ ⁿ e.

Some kids jump UP
as do flowers in spring,
some
        droop
            like
                wet clothes
                    on a line.

But I have been growing
book
by book
by book
by book

and I am turning out fine!

HUG

by Pat Mora

I like to hug
the people I love –
friends and family, I do.

I hug my pets.
I hug my dolls.
Hugging them is fun too.

When I hug my dad,
I shout,
"Daddy! Woo-hoo!"

I

INVENT

by Carol Labuzzetta

I found a box of old parts,
Tin cans, wires, and stuff to make art.

Without a book of directions or plans,
I've designed a robot with the cans.

I'm concentrating on the final task.
A turn of the screwdriver will make it last.

Trying to invent something takes time –
But, when it's done, it will be all mine!

J

JUMP

by Molly Lorenz

Jump like a cricket,
A lemur or squirrel.
A whale out of water,
A boy or a girl.

Jump into a puddle.
Jump over a log,
A crack in the sidewalk,
A rainbow or frog.

Just
Use
More
Push

JUMP!

KICK

by Janice Scully

Grass shaker
worm waker

High popper
cloud topper

Ball smasher
goal crasher

Tie breaker
score maker

Watch me
KICK!

LAUGH

by Jen Bryant

A tiny tee-hee
or full-out guffaw,
a belly-shaking chuckle,
or a *haw-haw-haw-HAW!!*
Launched from your heart
(where all good laughs start)
like thunder it rumbles,
lifts and tumbles
and bursts into the world!
So when you feel lonely
or sad or blue,
remember . . . *your* laugh
is right there for you!

MAKE

by Moe Phillips

You can make sand art in jelly jars
Make model planes and model cars
Paint flowers on a dish
Fold an origami fish
Make hand puppets out of socks
Make castles with building blocks
Sculpt a cat with molding clay

What will you make today?

NAP

by Padma Venkatraman

Do you like to jump like a jaguar,
bound like a bob cat,
prowl like a panther,
or leap like a lynx?

I'll tell you what I like to do.
I'm more cat-like than any of you.
I like to **nap** as long as I can,
curled up like a kitten in warm sunshine!

OPEN

by Linda Kulp Trout

I race my brother
down the sidewalk to the library,
each of us wanting to be first to go inside.

I'm way ahead, almost there
when I see a white-haired lady,
bag of books in one hand,
cane in the other.

I stop –
wait to open the door for her.
My brother charges by.
I don't mind.

I could've been first – but instead,
I choose to be kind.

PLAY

by Marilyn Garcia

All by myself
with this pile of toys
I sort them by color,
by shape, and by size,
stack them in towers
that reach to the sky.

When you sit beside me
and ask, "Can I play?"
We dream up new games
and we giggle together –
Good friends like *you*
make play even better.

QUACK

by Grace Lin

How do you do?
I ask.
QUACK!
the duck says to me.
What do you mean?
I ask.
QUACK!
the duck says to me.
Quack?
I ask.
QUACK!
the duck says to me.
So
QUACK! QUACK!
we say
to each other.

READ

by Margarita Engle

Please read with me
so we can see
winged horses
green forests
soaring heroes
dinosaur mysteries
and the brave history
of smart readers
like you
and me.

SIGN

by Marty Lapointe-Malchik

I'm learning to sign thank you.
That's what I want to say.
I touch my fingers to my chin,
Then tip my hand away.

Signing thanks one-handed
Is handy every day.
But signing thanks with both hands
Is like adding a bouquet.

T

TYPE

by Mary E. Cronin

I **type** a letter,
then another.
I **type** my name,
then my brother's.
Clickety tap . . .
the letters flow.
I **type** a list of words I know!

UNPACK

by Linda A. Dryfhout

Red, ripe tomatoes
and one purple plum,
yellow bananas
and blueberries, yum!

Leafy green broccoli,
melons to squeeze,
a bag of orange carrots,
a block of white cheese.

I unpack the groceries
we bought from the store.
There's a rainbow of color
behind our fridge door!

VISIT

by Helen Kemp Zax

When I visit my grandma
in winter and spring,
we build snowmen, drink cocoa,
find tadpoles, and swing.

When I visit my grandpa
in summer and fall,
we go swimming, pick berries,
fly kites, and play ball.

I couldn't go visit
for more than a year.
But the missing's gone missing . . .
now that I'm here!

WAVE

by Janet Clare Fagal

When we leave Grandma's,
she stands in the yard.

We get in our car.
I wave really hard.

Her smile is the sun.
My wave is the sky.

I wave from my window
for one more goodbye.

X-RAY

by Linda Sue Park

What's in your hand?

No –
inside
your hand

Let's X-RAY it to see. . . .

Your pinky bones
your thumb bones too!

Hey – let's X-RAY your knee!

YAWN

by Leslie Stall Widener

Three mothers chat,
with babies in cradleboards
worn on their backs.
Brown eyes peek out
of three round faces
with rosy cheeks.
They shut their eyes,
mouths open wide.
Nothing I can do.
I yawn, too.

Z

58

ZOOM

by Jone Rush MacCulloch

Helmet on
Time alone
Zoom, zoom, zoom

Pedal quick
Set the pace
Zoom, zoom, zoom

Shift the gears
Faster still
Zoom, zoom, zoom

Wheels whir
My world blurs –
ZOOM!

ABCDEFG

HIJK

LMNOP

QRSTUV

WXYZ

THE ALPHABET

by Janet Wong

You make a word with letters.
You build it as you go.
              C A N
That's right!
Your words will start to grow
into whole questions like:
       Can I have something sweet?

Or you might add extra letters
and make C A N a C A N D Y treat!

The alphabet is handy.
There are letters wherever you look:
on cereal boxes and all kinds of signs.
And, yes, of course, in a book!

RESOURCES
FOR
PARENTS
&
TEACHERS

TIPS FOR READERS

Here are some basic strategies for sharing poetry with children. Whether you're a family member, caregiver, teacher, librarian, or school administrator, these tips will help you get kids excited about reading!

Reading the pictures
With very young children, reading begins with everything EXCEPT the words. Encourage children to "read" or interpret the pictures and talk about what they see. They can even act out the key word like *dance, hug, jump*, or *wave*. Movement and play are an important part of learning too.

Reading aloud
Even if your child can read independently, it's good to hear poems read aloud for their sound qualities. Poems are meant to be read out loud to savor the words, sounds, and rhythm. Plus reading aloud together is a bonding time that makes reading a positive experience for young children just beginning to master the skills of reading.

Props and pantomime
Whether you're reading to a group of children or just one child, simple props or pantomime can make your read-aloud come alive. Use a common object mentioned in the poem as a "poetry prop," and hold it up while reading aloud. Or use gestures like raising your arm up when reading the poem "ASK"!

Combine listening and reading with echo reading
With echo reading, a child or a group of children will repeat lines of a poem after hearing you read them. Pause after each line and put a hand to your ear to cue your readers to repeat what they've just heard.

Point to words

Pointing to words as you read them is a great way to help children learn to read and helps them begin to associate the spoken word with the written word. It also reinforces the concept that English text moves from left to right, top to bottom.

Encourage guessing

Children often like rhyming poems because it's easy to guess the words that come at regular rhyming intervals. They sometimes will guess the wrong words, but it's good to encourage guessing; it makes reading feel like a game and builds prediction skills essential to comprehension.

Read parts

Some poems have a repeated word or phrase that you can point out before you start reading. You can read just the line with those repeated words before you read the whole poem. You don't need to read the whole poem each time!

Read, respond, and be open

Sometimes you'll want to talk to children to hear their reactions to a poem, but it's also fine just to read a poem and move on. If you do pause to chat, be open to their responses; children often notice surprising things and make unusual connections.

Record the reading

Record a poem to share with a friend or family member far away. It's easy to make an audio or video recording of a child reading either alone or together with you using your phone or an online tool such as Zoom or Google Meet. Or record yourself reading for your child to enjoy later when you may be away.

FUN ACTIVITIES TO TRY

Here are some activities for having fun with poetry in more creative ways after you've read and shared each poem.

Poem titles
Each poem has a one-word title and that word also appears in the poem itself and in a different color. This makes it easy for children to join in on that key word as you read the rest of the poem aloud and point to the word when it's their turn.

Learning letters
After reading the poem aloud, challenge children to think of other words that start with the same initial letter. For example, for A = Ask, you might offer *apple, alligator, art,* etc. Can you work together to think of other words that rhyme with the poem title word? For example, in B = Bend, the word *bend* rhymes with *end, send, mend, lend,* and so on.

Action
Every poem in this book focuses on an action word (or verb): *ask, bend, clap, dance, eat, fly, grow, hug, invent, jump, kick, laugh, make, nap, open, play, quack, read, sign, type, unpack, visit, wave, x-ray,* and *zoom.* Brainstorm more action words with children. Act them out and try making up a simple rhyme together.

Time for poetry
Reading a poem out loud takes less than a minute! Add a quick poem to your routine to build incidental literacy development. Start the day with a poem at breakfast, copy and add a poem to a lunch bag, or end the day with a poem read at dinner or at bedtime. Commemorate the first day of school with a poem, or the last day of school, or "moving up" day. You can also share a poem to celebrate a birthday.

Translate
Translate your favorite poem into another language spoken in your family or community. You can work with a friend or a neighbor or try GoogleTranslate to see how your poem sounds in French or Chinese or another language.

Poems in parts
Several poems in this book use italics (or quotation marks or all capital letters) for key words or phrases, which provides a helpful cue for reading a poem in parts. You can read most of the poem and then cue children to read the word or phrase in italics, quotes, or capitals. Try this approach with the poems *Ask, Dance, Play,* or *Quack.*

Body parts
Many of the poems in this book refer to body parts within the poem, such as in *Ask, Bend, Clap, Dance, Eat, Laugh, Sign,* and *Yawn.* Invite children to point to each body part as you read the poem out loud. This helps build large and small motor coordination.

Family poems
Several poems are about moments we share with our families. Work with children to share *Wave* or *Visit* with grandparents, *Unpack* or *Yawn* with parents and caregivers, and *Open* and *Type* with brothers or sisters.

Types of poems
There are several different types of poems in this book, some rhyming like *Kick* and some free verse or non-rhyming like *Quack.* Some have just a little bit of rhyme, like *Open.* One poem even has an acrostic built in (see the vertical letters that spell JUMP in *Jump*). Challenge children to use their names (or other words) to write their own acrostic poem.

WEB RESOURCES

There are so many useful literacy resources online that it's sometimes hard to know where to start. You'll find basic information and engaging activities at the following recommended websites. Dive in and have fun!

CDBD: patmora.com/whats-childrens-day-book-day/
Children's Day, Book Day (CDBD or Día) is a nationally recognized initiative celebrated all year and culminating on April 30th. It emphasizes the importance of literacy for all children from all backgrounds.

colorincolorado.org
Colorín Colorado is a national multimedia project that offers bilingual activities and advice for educators and families of English language learners (ELLs).

everychildareader.net
Every Child a Reader connects book creators with learning communities, providing literacy tools and resources. Their many outreach programs include the Kids' Book Choice Awards.

ibby.org
The International Board on Books for Young People (IBBY) is an international network with dozens of chapters all over the world working together to connect children with books.

kidlit.tv
KidLit TV creates videos that highlight brand new books and the authors and illustrators who created them. They also offer arts and crafts activities and live coverage of special literary events.

naeyc.org
The National Association for the Education of Young Children (NAEYC) is a membership organization that provides professional development and support for early childhood educators and families.

reachoutandread.org
Endorsed by the American Academy of Pediatrics (AAP), this site provides early literacy tools in Spanish, screen-free activities, and links to even more resources for reading with children.

readingrockets.org
Reading Rockets is an education initiative of the public television station WETA. In their "Reading Topics A-Z" you can find online resources on autism, dyslexia, and much more.

thebrownbookshelf.com
The Brown Bookshelf amplifies Black stories and sponsors "28 Days Later," a showcase of picture books and novels for young readers by Black authors and illustrators.

usbby.org
The United States Board on Books for Young People (USBBY) is the U.S. national section of IBBY, with an Outstanding International Books List that features titles for children that promote global understanding.

WNDB: diversebooks.org
We Need Diverse Books (WNDB) is a grassroots organization with resources on race, equity, anti-racism, and inclusion. Their mission is putting more books with diverse characters into the hands of all children.

ABOUT THE POETS

You probably found some favorite poems when reading this book. Write down the poets' names and learn more about them by visiting their websites and blogs. Then look for more of their poems (and books)!

Beth Brody   bethbrodywriter.net
Beth Brody writes picture books and poetry and is currently working on historical novels in verse. The garden, not the yoga mat, is where she bends and stretches and opens up her heart.

Joseph Bruchac   josephbruchac.com
Joseph Bruchac is the author of more than 170 books for children and adults, including *Rabbit's Snow Dance*, a modern retelling of an Iroquois folktale. When he's happy (and he knows it), he claps his hands.

Jen Bryant   jenbryant.com
Jen Bryant is the author of many award-winning books, especially picture book biographies such as *SIX DOTS: A Story of Young Louis Braille.* When she is not laughing, she is often (at least) smiling.

Mary E. Cronin   maryecronin.com
Mary E. Cronin is a K-2 Literacy Coach whose poetry and essays have appeared in many publications including *The New York Times*. She loves to type up poems on her computer.

Linda A. Dryfhout   Twitter: @LADryfhout
Linda A. Dryfhout is a poet whose work has appeared in magazines and in anthologies such as *The Poetry Friday Anthology for Celebrations*. She loves unpacking her suitcase when visiting her grandchildren.

Margarita Engle   margaritaengle.com
Margarita Engle is the Cuban American author of more than thirty
award-winning verse novels, memoirs, and picture books, including *Light
for All*. She spends hours in her local bookstore, finding books to read.

Janet Clare Fagal   Twitter: @skanlaker
Janet Clare Fagal was a teacher for 40 years before she became a
published poet. Her passion is encouraging children to learn poems by
heart. You can find her waving hello and goodbye to her grandchildren.

Marilyn Garcia   marilynrgarcia.com
Marilyn Garcia is a poet whose many activities include beekeeping. Her
work has appeared in anthologies such as *HOP TO IT: Poems to Get You
Moving*. She enjoys playing with her family and their many cats.

Nikki Grimes   nikkigrimes.com
Nikki Grimes has won numerous awards for her poetry, novels, memoir,
biographies, and picture books about everyday topics, such as *Off to See
the Sea*. She likes to look up at the sky and watch the clouds dancing.

Carol Labuzzetta   theapplesinmyorchard.com
Carol Labuzzetta is a writer, advocate for talented and gifted (TAG)
children, citizen scientist, and environmental educator. Many people in
her family like to invent things.

Marty Lapointe-Malchik   imarty.com
Marty Lapointe-Malchik is a poet and collage artist who works with
children who are deaf (and their families). A deaf colleague taught her to
show extra thanks with the two-handed sign for thank you.

Grace Lin   gracelin.com
Grace Lin has won both Newbery and Caldecott Honors (*Where the Mountain Meets the Moon* and *A Big Mooncake for Little Star*). Quacking is often heard at Grace's house, as her family loves ducks.

Molly Lorenz   Twitter: @booksR4me
Molly Lorenz is a member of SCBWI and has been an art educator, creative problem solver, artist, quilter, and writer. When she spends time with her granddaughter, jumping is often at the top of the list.

Jone Rush MacCulloch   jonerushmacculloch.com
Jone Rush MacCulloch is a former library media specialist and teacher who is a poet, photographer, and Poetry Friday blogger. You can see her zooming around town, walking, and zooming in on nature with her camera.

Pat Mora   patmora.com
Pat Mora's many books make us happy, especially *Bookjoy, Wordjoy*, a celebration of wordplay. Pat is the founder of Children's Day, Book Day (also known as Día; see p. 68). She loves to hug her family and friends.

Linda Sue Park   lindasuepark.com
Linda Sue Park is a Newbery winner (*A Single Shard*) who has won hundreds of awards and commendations. Her book *Gurple and Preen* is about broken crayons. If you ever think you have broken something, get an X-ray!

Moe Phillips   moephillips.com
Moe Phillips is a writer and film producer who is also an avid birder and volunteer for wildlife rehabilitation. She loves to make fairy forts in her garden with logs, branches, leaves, and rocks.

Jack Prelutsky   poetryfoundation.org/poets/jack-prelutsky
Jack Prelutsky is one of the most prolific children's poets in the world. He has created more than 70 children's poetry books, including *Hard-Boiled Bugs for Breakfast: And Other Tasty Poems*. He loves to eat.

Janice Scully   janicescully.com
Janice Scully is a retired physician who writes for children and grew up living over her family's busy restaurant. When on a long walk, she can sometimes be found kicking a rock.

Linda Kulp Trout   lindakulptrout.blogspot.com
Linda Kulp Trout is a retired teacher whose poems, short stories, and articles have appeared in many publications. She loves to visit the library, and often holds the door open to help people.

Padma Venkatraman   padmavenkatraman.com
Padma Venkatraman worked as chief scientist on research vessels before becoming the author of novels such as *Born Behind Bars*. One of her favorite places to catnap is in warm sunshine on a ship at sea.

Carole Boston Weatherford   cbweatherford.com
Carole Boston Weatherford's books have won Caldecott Honors, NAACP Image Awards, and an SCBWI Golden Kite Award. *You Can Fly: The Tuskegee Airmen* was created with her son, artist Jeffery Weatherford.

Leslie Stall Widener   lesliestallwidener.com
Leslie Stall Widener is a member of the Choctaw Nation of Oklahoma. She is a poet as well as the illustrator of Choctaw tales such as *Chukfi Rabbit's Big, Bad Bellyache: A Trickster Tale*. She loves yawning babies.

Jane Yolen   janeyolen.com
Jane Yolen is the author of over 400 books, including *EEK, YOU REEK!: Poems about Animals That Stink, Stank, Stunk*, written with her daughter Heidi E. Y. Stemple. She loves seeing her grandchildren grow.

Helen Kemp Zax   Twitter: @HelenZax
Helen Kemp Zax is a former lawyer whose poems have been published in anthologies such as *HOP TO IT: Poems to Get You Moving*. She often misses her children and always enjoys their visits.

POEM CREDITS

ABOUT VARDELL & WONG

Sylvia M. Vardell is Professor in the School of Library and Information Studies at Texas Woman's University and teaches graduate courses in children's and young adult literature. Vardell has published extensively, including five books on literature for children as well as over 25 book chapters and 100 journal articles. In 2020, she curated the anthology *A World Full of Poems: Inspiring Poetry for Children*. One of the things she loves to do is cuddle with her rescue dog Wilby. Learn more about her at SylviaVardell.com.

Janet Wong is a graduate of Yale Law School and a former lawyer. She has written more than 35 books for children on a wide variety of subjects, including chess (*Alex and the Wednesday Chess Club*) and yoga (*TWIST: Yoga Poems*). She is the 2021 winner of the NCTE Excellence in Poetry for Children Award, a lifetime achievement award that is one of the highest honors a children's poet can receive. One of her favorite things to do is to eat, and she often eats two lunches on the same day. Learn more about her at JanetWong.com.

Together, Vardell & Wong are the creative forces behind Pomelo Books.

ABOUT POMELO BOOKS

Pomelo Books is Poetry PLUS. Poetry PLUS play. Poetry PLUS science. Poetry PLUS holidays. Poetry PLUS pets — and more. We make it EASY to share poetry any time of day!

Successful K-12 teachers and administrators build regular "touch points" into their routines to create a safe and engaging learning environment. Poetry can be a powerful tool for offering a shared literary experience in just a few minutes, with both curricular benefits and emotional connections for students at all levels.

Our books in The Poetry Friday Anthology series and the Poetry Friday Power Book series make it easy to use poetry for integrating skills, building language learning, crossing curricular areas, mentoring young writers, promoting critical thinking, fostering social-emotional development, and inviting students to respond creatively.

A shared poetry moment can help build a classroom community filled with kindness, respect, and joy. Learn more at PomeloBooks.com.

OTHER BOOKS BY
VARDELL & WONG

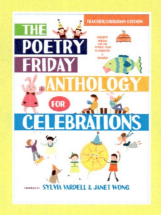

The Poetry Friday Anthology for Celebrations
ILA Notable Books for a Global Society

This fun book features 156 poems (in both Spanish & English) honoring a wide variety of traditional and non-traditional holidays from all over the world. (Also available in a Teacher/Librarian Edition.)

"A bubbly and educational bilingual poetry anthology for children." – Kirkus

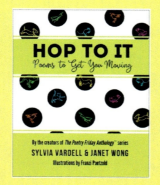

Hop to It: Poems to Get You Moving
A KBCA "Best Book of Facts" Finalist

This anthology of 100 poems by 90 poets gets kids thinking and moving as they use pantomime, sign language, and whole body movements, including deskercise! You'll also find poems on current topics, such as life during a pandemic. Take a 30-second indoor recess whenever you need it!

Pet Crazy: A Poetry Friday Power Book
A CBC Hot Off the Press selection

This interactive story – with Hidden Language Skills that engage kids in "playing" with punctuation, spelling, and other basics – features three characters who love spending time with animals. Extensive back matter features resources for helping young people perform, read, write, and try to publish poetry.

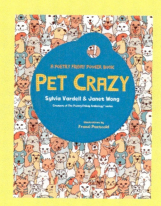

"An enthusiastic invitation for kids to celebrate their animal friends through poetry composition." – Kirkus

The Poetry of Science
An NSTA Recommends selection

The Poetry of Science is an illustrated book for children that contains 250 poems on science, technology, engineering, and math organized by topic. (A companion Teacher/Librarian Edition features mini-lessons and resources).

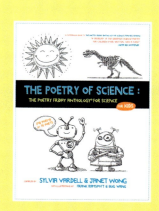

"A treasury of the greatest science poetry for children ever written, with a twist." – NSTA

Made in the USA
Coppell, TX
25 October 2021